# The Moon And The Shopping Cart

## A Book Of Poems

Sean Early

BookLeaf Publishing

India | USA | UK

Made with ❤ on the BookLeaf Publishing Platform
www.bookleafpub.in
www.bookleafpub.com

# Dedication

for sage and elsie

# Preface

The following text was written and compiled over the length of about six years. They began, in part, as a way to explain myself and our world to my daughter when she comes looking for answers in her late teens. I'm not sure I succeeded in my initial goal.
These words represent my faith, my fears and my frustrations in the world around me. These words are that of the American condition as it I've found it, like an old Honda long since abandoned beside a shady country lane with her windows smashed out and all her doors ripped open taking on water and moss and plants. Fragments of these poems have become lyrics in songs, but they appear here in their original form as first intended. There are several literary references plucked directly from classics within these pages. If you figure out what they are, come find me. We'll talk it out and I'll buy you a coffee. Just don't spoil it for everyone else.
Sincerely,
Sean Early
January 2025,
Litchfield CT.

# Acknowledgements

First I'd like to take this time to thank you, dear reader, for purchasing this independent book. Thank you in advance for taking your time with these words. Let them linger in your heart like steeping tea. Contemplate them while you walk in the place you most feel whole, wherever that may be.

I'd like to express my sincerest gratitude to every teacher who ever gave me shelter from the storm, those who gave me a place to hide, each of those who kept a queer kid out of trouble when they could help it.

Lastly and very simply I'd like to thank my family, both chosen and blood, for giving me the opportunity to express myself as I choose fit. Thank you for embracing me as the absolute Muppet of a human I've always been. Please be good to each other. We are all that we have.

Sean Early

February 2025

Litchfield, CT

# 1. All The Hills Ablaze

Council yourself.
Triage your purpose.
Throw punches in the dark
at your memories.
All the hills ablaze.
A thousand crows spot the sky.
Plastic corn grows wild.
This is not a hill to die on but
it is a hill nonetheless.
All them ablaze.
Model actress actress model
"Get your memories off of me"
Hold your tongue was
the advice you gave.
A flawed and lasting legacy.

# 2. A Public Execution

Give your heels wings
into the shelter of the wood
Peasants swarm
A world of noise
Face as grey as ashes
Bitter laws of
Them who be guilty.
All the while
Even the hangman
Turned away.
Charge it all up to profit
and loss.
Clasped her hands.
The sheriff
 has no friend.

# 3. The Greenest Bottle

There is a lone green glass beer bottle at the very bottom
 of the Mariana Trench, I often lose time thinking about
it. For six miles and change it sunk further, unelected of
and against its own volition into the pressurized depths
of silt and rot.
Had it drifted from a beach? Had it been flung from a
fishing boat? Had a kind hearted fool of a tourist
knocked it off a pier in Kauai? Was it the first tasty
beverage of the night or the last shameful one?
Who's to say.
I find myself in shopping lines thinking about this
bottle. I find myself in the throws of
important conversations and I will wonder what glass
does in such a state.
Is it still glass? Or just neatly stacked green sand?
Will the softest current shatter its brittle form?
Or has it taken on a different state,
like orange juice in a weightless space?

# 4. Soup in a Heatwave

Apprehend the sherif
Wax mannequins
melting in a heatwave.
Defrock the cardinal.
Phantom breaking
from the passenger seat
A fiberglass hull in
 a late summers squall
green water making its
presence and strength known,
pouring over the sides
as our vessel tacks in
strategic desperation.
My earliest memory
is being convinced
I was about to drown.

# 5. Mail Order Congressman

Meeting Notes Email Draft
Tiny Jars Who Even Knows Who
Take Me Apart & Lose The Pieces Sixteen Years
Cafeteria Trays Gossip Goblins Spit It Out
Wicked Nuns. Who Ate My Sandwich?
Is This A Good Place For A Poet To Sleep?
Hey, I've Been There. Oil Paint Smells Like
You Know What You're Getting Good At This.
Dump Me In A Swamp. Remember. Remember.
First Class Scumbag. Slumlord On Rikers Island
All Of These Idea Machines And No Ideas
Woody's Everlasting Hellscape Realized
Bovine Implants. Sure, It's Lovely, But Is It Buoyant?
 Princess On The Moon. Mail Order Congressman
Vacuum Solo. Mom's Gonna Be Pissed
A Month And Some Change Dead Wrong
 At The Palace Gates Who Even Goes To These Things?

# 6. Wet Dog In The Summer

Take a walk in the tall grass,
where the tests go ungraded.

Go climb a tree and leave your
phone unattended,
overheating in the sun.

Unsnap the rubberband of your soul.

Just a wet dog in the summer wheat.
The whole world sticking to my stubborn knees.
Starting over fresh at the end of the week.
We traded clothes in your Volvo
You bought me something to eat.

# 7. The Safecrack & The Diplomat

They continue without us all the same.
The woods will always be there.
And that city is older than dirt.
Neither holy nor an empire.
Knocking down the past.
Make way for progress,
said the safecrack to the diplomat.
Teenagers riding the
tops of subway cars for clout.
Stop talking about yesterday,
I think we've heard enough, miss.
That's an awfully nice coffin
you've built for us all.
Hopes and dreams and
the scratch off machine.

# 8. Yurik's Lament

My Lord, he likes a pretty song.
Like humming to unseen songbirds
 and accepting collect calls from strangers,
like children eating everything
 bagels with the seeds removed.
Paint left to dry with the lid ajar.
Drinking turpentine for the taste.
We'll turn our fine just how we are.
Palace intrigue. Staying busy.
We've got spies to find informants.
Informants to find more spies.
One us isn't us any longer.
Like smoke from fires unseen.
Like punishment for dreams.
Like hearing helicopters over
the next valley and knowing
that you'll see them if you wait.
Like cutting off your fingers for forgiveness.
Like grass growing and dying
without ever having served a purpose.
Lately I've been running
out of jokes to tell the king.

# 9. Of The Woods

Be swift, go forth.
Go find yourself amongst the ticks.
Unclench your jaw and go feral.
Don't believe a word the wolf has to say.
He'll rock paper scissor
you for your mortal soul.
The sower follows the
scorched earth like
the vulture trails the fox
in the endless summer heat.
The light will eat the shadows
and borrow all your dreams.
Like smoking in a bathroom.
Like eating off the floor.
Dig your feet in and push.
Do you know who knit your sweater?
You should gift it to the wolf, it
would fit him much better.

# 10. Dancing On The Radiator

Smell holds firm to memory.
Like asbestos in your lungs.
A dank center console on a
warm summer road,
windows rolled down
taking in the breeze.
Rotting leather trim in an otherwise
well kept truck, slowly gathering
airborn salt on the side of the road
as it permeates every-which-way,
its aim unknowable, but one would
assume it's aim still true.
Road sodas for the boat are
boat sodas, everyone knows that.
Swimming off the coast of Plum Island.
Dancing on the radiator.
Death opens a portal, she says.
Recording songs off the radio.
Smoking with the windows rolled up.
Cars look to me like the people who own them.
Borrowing change from strangers cars.
You gave me the silent treatment
for all that summer, I was fine.

# 11. All That Never Was

While the troopers were burning ballots
the troubadours were writing ballads
Peace and justice were subverted
in the name of steady balance.

Who am I to judge their them?
Who are you to weigh a soul?
Theres youth pastors in camo
playing soldier in the road.

Oldest story to imagine.
The queen, I heard her laughing.
The jester he saw everything,
there's been another stabbing.

Ode to all that never was
in the shopping cart of your heart.
I watched you flee the palace
when the peasants got their start.

# 12. Scapegoat Season

There isn't much to time travel,
it's just folding leaves of grass.
Good old boys in pick up trucks
all hate what they can't grasp.
I'm you, you know.
I'm everything you push aside
in the downstairs of your soul.

It's scapegoat season once again.
They're waiving banners,
wearings masks.
Telling other citizens
that they're more citizen than they.

All hail the burnout king.
He knows all the shortcuts.

# 13. Portrait Of Death

The teeth of time are made of stone.
They chew through metal.
They chew through flesh.
They chew bone and memory
and plastic and empires
and untold legions shaking in the mud.

The teeth of time are made of stone.
They crush neighborhoods.
They eat factories and labor parties.
The perpetual landslide of fiscal growth
is born on the backs of the serfs and their phones.

I sat on my cart, with my dog and my mule
and watched a mountain burn in the distance.
Not one of us said a word.
The fire glowed and like a brilliant
billboard from an angry god
drunk off of rage and indifference.

# 14. Hey Norman Rockwell

Fold me like a letter
that you want to read again.
The sky is raining satellites,
igniting on reentry like
ballerinas soaked in kerosene.
Kill your regional accent out of
fear someone might know you.
God forbid anyone ever know you.
But me? I come from a long line of
rabbit eaters and horse thieves
and unlicensed apothecaries.
Time is a mushy bowl of cereal.
Did you know you can start an
old Honda with a flathead screwdriver?
The sky is raining satellites,
swamps are hard to drain.

# 15. Go Tell The King

Behold! A mighty
liar and magician.
Footsteps coming.
Make haste you twat
Go tell the king
 I will blot out the sun.
Turn thee cold.
In that great triumph,
For lack of light and warmth,
In their vast concrete nothing
I will stand amongst thee
and recite their weary deeds.
Whilst I was shooting dice
with princes who pat me
on the back bottle in hand,
them forever laughing saying
"I've stabbed better
men than you."
Such fortunate fools
waiving banners
Smoking cigars
in celebration of
 their own undoing.

# 16. The Moon & The Shopping Cart

There's more than one way to skin a cat.
The Dread Pirate Roberts was pardoned
this morning. "You're paying too much attention."
Overwhelm the masses. Flood the courts.
Qualified immunity. Oligarchical practices,
sneering at the pulpit while
the bishop begs for mercy.
Everything was forever, you said.
Didn't seem to last too long though.
Puritan clerical siegecraft; a talk on
fortresses and how to bombard them.
I got some opium from a GI on furlough.
I am Jimmy Stewart carpet bombing Europe,
watching drone warfare on my phone
while I eat my microwaved croissant.

# 17. From The Nosebleeds

Some horses are for racing.
Some horses are for meat.
Compare yourself to everyone
on the computer.
Cling to your government.
Climb through your family.
Claw at the walls
in your grief and your rage.
Some rivers are for drinking.
Some rivers are poisoned.
Sometimes water is flammable.
Lets cross the double line,
passing three cars at a time.
Let's play scrabble for our lives.

# 18. A Goat Plays Chess

Hey, I've been there.
Future moss food, headed nowhere.
The jester's are doing parlor tricks,
making powders disappear.
Lets all watch a pope bend the knee,
I hope they'll be serving dessert soon.
The holy goat was left to graze on our
intentions and well wishes which were
strewn about like aircraft parts
raining down on us at random.
Their love is conditional, don't you see?
Thy love is a chainsaw on autopilot.
No one here knows how to actually play chess.
If you've anything to say at all
you should say it with your chest.

www.ingramcontent.com/pod-product-compliance
Lightning Source LLC
LaVergne TN
LVHW050303200726